Teacher-Parent Relationships

Jeannette Galambos Stone

National Association for the Education of Young Children
1834 Connecticut Avenue, N.W.
Washington, D.C. 20009-5786

A 1987–88 Comprehensive Membership Benefit

National Association for the Education of Young Children
1834 Connecticut Avenue, N.W.
Washington, DC 20009-5786
202-232-8777   800-424-2460

Library of Congress Card Catalog Number: 87-062636
ISBN 0-935989-10-2
NAEYC #226

Foreword

I want to express my appreciation to the director and the teachers of the Leila Day Nursery, a child care center in New Haven, Connecticut, for their generosity of time and spirit. In the most professional way, they reviewed teacher-parent relationships with me and gave of their wisdom and experience.

I would also like to thank the director and staff of the Charlie Mills Preschool in Branford, Connecticut. They, too, shared information and philosophy with me.

For several decades I have been reading research findings on teacher-parent connections and activities, though I have not conducted research myself. In large part, in preparing this booklet, I have drawn on my experiences as a preschool teacher and consultant from 1954 through the present in co-op and community nursery schools, Head Start, infant and child care centers, special education, and both public and private kindergartens. Finally, my own grown children and their children (all veterans of infant-toddler programs and day care) have taught me a lot.

Some writings on parents and teachers have stated — I think unrealistically — that "we all want the best for our children" without coming to grips with the fact that people usually disagree on what "the best" is. I hope, in this booklet, to present ways that various parents and teachers have found helpful when coping with differing views, needs, and life experiences. For their contributions I am very grateful.

Note to the Reader

T his booklet deals with teachers and parents reacting to children and to each other during their first moments together in children's centers and then during their many contacts there — which, along with conferences and meetings, account for almost all of the time they spend in each other's company.

I hope you will accept my use of the words *she* and *her* when alluding to teachers. Though occasionally I meet male preschool teachers, most are female still. So, in the interest of simplicity, I have indicated female gender. At any rate, I think that male and female teachers have similar experiences working with parents of young children, and this is borne out in my conversations with those men I have met working in child care.

In referring to group settings for young children, I speak of centers, schools, and preschools, all interchangeably. I hope that people from all settings will find this booklet relevant and useful whether in family day care, nursery school, Head Start, infant and child care centers, after-school programs, special education preschools, or primary classrooms.

Finally, with the word *teacher,* I mean the various adults who work with children in these centers, including administrators, head teachers, assistants, aides, and volunteers. Young children are influenced by all adults taking care of them.

Just as my colleagues and I have looked back on our experiences as teachers and parents in order to clarify our positions, I urge you to reflect on your experiences and emerge with practical and wise positions of your own on teacher-parent relationships.

The Purpose of This Booklet

My purpose here is to present the value (and practicality) of open-minded, untiring efforts by parents and teachers to listen to each other and to keep trying to work together. I think in terms of *adult education* rather than parent education. *Parents and teachers educate each other during open two-way communication when each tries to meet the other at least halfway.* Parents thus inform teachers about their own child; they are gold mines of information and insight. Teachers inform parents about child development and preschool curriculum, and about how *this* child copes and learns in a group setting. Each point of view enlightens the other.

How can we find more and better ways to do this? What sorts of mix-ups and discourtesies get in the way? Of course, some teacher-parent relationships go easily and are marked by mutual respect and enjoyment. Many others are mixed but go along smoothly enough so that satisfaction outweighs discomfort. But in troubled relationships, both teachers and parents may find that greetings and good-byes, informal conversation, and attempts at serious discussion become heavy with tension — and with heated words or silent resentment. Instead of thinking in terms of opposing sides, with an "us-versus-them" stance, parents and teachers need to find ways to share information and to speak openly and effectively throughout everyday contacts and during conferences. This booklet includes ideas for such exchanges as well as suggestions for examining others' points of view without compromising our own convictions.

Teacher-parent relationships are built in slow steps. They form in subtle ways from the very beginnings of enrollment, as parents ask their first questions about a child care center or nursery school for their child (usually by telephone) and then arrange a visit to see the program and meet the staff. Teachers and administrators are taking professional care of children because parents entrust their children to them. Parents want information: Is this a good program? Are the teachers trained and professional? . . . kind? . . . attentive? Do they like children? Will they have time for parents? Are classrooms and outdoor areas safe and clean? Does the center meet local and state guidelines?

As parents make that first call to a center, they listen hard, and they hear not only the answers to their questions but also the tone in which the secretary or director speaks to them — with warmth and careful attention, or without. Parents' impressions of that conversation form the first steps — permanent steps — of their relationship with the school.

Next, a brochure, mailed or handed to the family, will strengthen the relationship if
- its tone is friendly and its pages interesting,
- it is full of facts — and pictures that bring the facts to life, and
- it invites parents to make an appointment to visit the center — making clear whether or not the child comes along for this first visit.

First Steps

First questions

The tone is set

Subjects & Predicates

Parents' first impression of a school is usually formed from a phone call for information about the program. Warmth and careful attention from the person they speak to are as important as the answers to their questions.

First meeting

Visit to the classroom

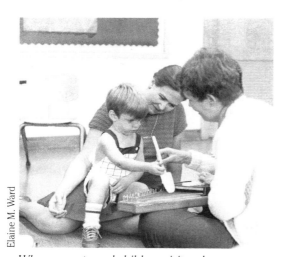

When parents and children visit a classroom before enrollment, the teacher must make them feel comfortable. Let them know if they should merely observe or are welcome to join in class activities — and let the child decide if he's ready to join in, or if he needs to stay back and just take it all in.

Elaine M. Ward

Now comes the meeting of parent, director and/or teacher, and in some cases the child as well. In this step, parents want to check their impressions, and the director wants to make sure that the school is a good match for the child and family.

Helping parents feel at ease is an art. Providing comfortable chairs and coffee or juice in the interview room and providing enough time for talking and for looking at the classroom are part of the art. Offering toys to the visiting child is part of the art, too; of course, it's the child's choice whether to play with the toys or to stay perched on her mother's lap.

Let's say we go to the next step: a visit to the classroom. A warm welcome by the teacher is crucial. She comes forward to greet the visitors by name, chats with them, points out the play/work areas of the room, introduces them very briefly and casually to the class. She neither interrupts the class with loud introductions that embarrass the visitors, nor neglects to acknowledge their presence. The teacher then leads them to chairs where they can settle in and observe. The child is gently invited to enter the play or not as he feels comfortable. The teacher will need to return to the other children; she excuses herself, suggesting that the parents save their questions, for her or the director, to be answered later. Some centers give parents a visitors' guide sheet with suggestions for observing — whether to speak to children in the class and whether to walk around or stay put. From printed or spoken suggestions, parents know what is expected.

It helps, too, if the teacher neither ignores her visitors nor insists on the child's answering questions or joining activities. The visitors need time and space to take it all in, to get the feel of the place, and should be treated as guests — with respect for and awareness of how they are feeling during the visit.

The classroom visit is followed by a talk between parents and director to check impressions. Waiting lists and priorities are spelled out, and enrollment procedures reviewed. The director makes sure she describes the basic educational approach in the center.

Occasionally a special-needs child, or a child troubled by some physical or psychological problem, is considered for acceptance. If either the parent or director feels some caution or hesitation, the director may want to suggest that, if enrolled, the child attend on a trial basis. Also, the director might describe the school's occasional use of state or local consultants, who are available in most locations to help both families and teachers. (Every city and county in this country has health, mental health, and social services departments. Look under city or county listings in your phone book.)

Enrollment is proceeding step by step. Staff and parents talk about their goals and think out loud together, sharing as much information as possible. Some parents want to look at other centers; then, the director suggests alternatives, and the parents' search continues. Or the parents might need a second visit in this program.

The director and teachers plan to observe each child applicant — during a classroom visit arranged for that purpose, or during a small gathering of new children who can play together for a few minutes (perhaps on a Saturday) while parents and teachers try to assess the match of school and child. The parent may have visited a number of programs that turned out to have no vacancies, or that had little appeal.

After sufficient visiting and discussion, the director completes enrollment. She lets each parent know whether her or his child has been accepted or placed on a waiting list . . . and where on the list. And she describes the next steps to be taken.

Once the director informs parents that their child is "in," forms are completed — medical forms, permission forms. Parent, child, and teacher are launched. How can they be helped to work well together?

Many preschool teachers believe fervently in taking time to make

Explanations

Special procedures

Application and enrollment: The long process

Final steps

Home visits

home visits before the child starts school, especially if the child is a young toddler or a 2- or 3-year-old. The teacher calls for a time to visit, making sure that the parent understands why she is coming — that a home visit is not meant to look over the house or apartment, but to help the child get to know her teacher and look forward to coming to school. During this brief visit, the child has a chance to show her new teacher her favorite book or toy, or her bed, or TV — whatever she wants to show. The teacher answers last-minute questions about the program and gives the parent any printed information about children's clothing at school, birthday celebrations, and procedures in case the child gets sick.

The child has not yet started school, but many vital steps have been taken that will affect parents' satisfaction with the program. If all has gone well, parents feel assured that their child will have a safe, nurturing, interesting time there.

Even before a child has started school, many vital steps have been taken to assure parents that their child will have a safe, nurturing, interesting time there.

Ginger Howard

Children and parents love and need each other, and separating from one another can be painful, even though it's exciting and challenging. Separation from family is going to go on, in one way or another, throughout all of life. It is almost always very hard. Children appear to move into group life more easily when they have time to get used to the idea. To expect toddlers and 3s (even 4s) to wave off their parents without a pang is to fly in the face of common sense.

To be sure, some children *do* wave Mom off the first day; some regret their haste and decide, days or weeks later, that they want her back in school with them. Some need Mommy or Dad to stay the first day, then feel OK on their own.

However, there are children who feel especially uneasy about separating from family. These children are not necessarily immature or overdependent. They may simply feel deeply rooted and bonded. They love their parents unabashedly and feel stricken when separated from them. They may grow up to become adults of unusual depth and strength of character. At any rate, they need patience and good humor now, when they're starting family day care, or nursery school, or Head Start, or child care, or kindergarten, or another type of program. They may react to being left at the center by screaming or by retreating, mute and limp, to a corner or cubby. Teachers are hard put to reassure and comfort these children and, at the same time, to provide a pleasant, busy classroom for the others. But they try.

It saves wear and tear if Mom or Dad (or Grandma) stays at the center with the upset or sad child for part of the first day, the whole day, or even several days. Because successfully separating is so important in the lives of young children, even though being at work is important for parents, it is strongly recommended that parents take time off when their child starts school. No grown-up is as good as a parent or grandparent at a time like this. Parents may resist —

Ready To Start: Separation

Separation

Michael Schulman

Children need time to become independent. Children are less likely to become upset if Mom or Dad (or Grandma) stays at the center for part of the first day.

5

Staying with a child

some because of difficulty arranging time off from work, some because they think their child should be more independent. Isn't it possible, though, that little children need *time* to become independent, and that they would be more successful if their parents and teachers did not force a sudden break but rather eased them through the transition for a few days? Or even just for the first day?

One excellent child care center in the New York area *requires* a parent to stay with his or her child for the first day. The parent arranges the necessary but brief time off. In that center, beginning days of school go quite smoothly for child, parent, and teacher. Parents *do* take time off because the wise director has the courage to expect everyone involved to do what's best for the child.

A child's sense of the passage of time is sketchy. She's not sure: How long will she be here? Will she be OK? Will the teacher be nice to her? Will Dad come back for sure? When *is* the "end of the day"?

The teacher befriends

Let's imagine a good scenario for a child. The teacher keeps an eye on him, smiles at him, pats him gently on the shoulder, offers a puzzle or some markers and paper, or a place at the play dough table, or a chance to feed the pet rabbit. She doesn't get prickly if the child refuses her offerings and chooses instead to stand on the sidelines. This teacher will come by from time to time, casually checking in with the child; she might place a toy truck or a book nearby, offer juice and crackers on a reachable table if he doesn't want to join the other children for snack. This teacher *befriends* the child — not chiding, not ignoring, not taking his standoffish behavior personally. She understands, and accepts him as he is.

All of this is part of the art of teaching: reassuring, motivating, befriending.

The teacher helps

A teacher can help a child through separation by picking him up when his mother leaves the center, taking him to a window to wave good-bye, then accompanying him to an activity — working on a puzzle or watering the plants. Scolding or chiding ruin any budding feelings in the child of trust and belonging. To say "Now don't act like a baby" is not only unprofessional but pointless. It doesn't help. This would work better: "I know you want your Mom. . . . She is going to go to work, isn't she? She'll be back after your nap, Sam. I'll help you manage! Let's go over to the table and make something. . . . Maria is there, too. Maria, can you pass Sam that paste brush and the scissors?"

There are tried-and-true techniques that help when Mom has to leave a clinging child. Mom and 3-year-old Shauna have been sitting at a table, Shauna working on puzzles and watching the other children. After morning snack and by agreement with the teacher — who has discussed departure strategies with the parent in advance — Mom tells Shauna that she's going to the store for groceries and Shauna will stay at school. Shauna's face breaks apart. She clutches her mother and begins to cry. Teacher edges over now, available for what is coming. Mom stands up, goes to the hall to get her jacket. Shauna howls. Mom returns to her, says good-bye. Teacher shows Shauna the clock: "Mom will be back around noon. She's going to the supermarket." Mom kisses Shauna, leaves — not changing her mind, not asking Shauna "Is it OK?" (It's not her choice.) Shauna cries hard. Teacher copes, staying with her, holding her if she lets her, reading to her, or taking her with her as she helps other children in the block area, at the easel, and during clean-up. Mom returns soon with the groceries, stays on for nap and outdoor play. Next day she makes the break, leaving in the morning for work, telling Shauna that she will be back, like yesterday, and that Shauna will have things to do at school. With the teacher's support (even coaching), Mom makes a real effort to come across as steady, firm, sure. This is easier for some mothers than for others. Shauna may recover in a few minutes, or she may cry for a long time. This is very hard on busy teachers, and especially on new teachers who haven't weathered such storms before.

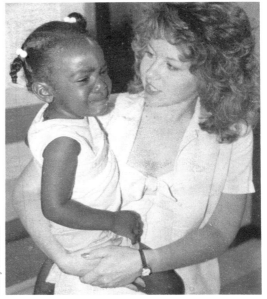

Nancy Alexander

The teacher can help a child who misses her parent by staying with her, holding her if she lets her, reading to her, or taking her with her as she helps other children around the room.

A quick trial run

The final break

Calls and notes

Children who are given plenty of time and space for free play will be able to cast off their preoccupation with home and get into pretend play in the housekeeping corner, or with puppets, or out in the yard.

What do children learn about being on their own?

Help from teachers

Teachers at some centers allow a sad or upset child to call a parent by telephone (at home, even at work) for contact and reassurance. Other teachers have offered, with great results, to write "notes" for the children. I learned about "notes" from Barbara Steinau, the director of the Charlie Mills Preschool. She came up with the idea in response to an unhappy child and has used it for many other children since. Other teachers elsewhere probably have had the same idea. . . . Four-year-old Terry is distraught after her father leaves her at the center. Mommy is in the hospital.

Teacher: "You're having a pretty hard time. Would it help if I wrote a note from you to your father?"

The child almost always likes this idea and says yes through the tears.

Teacher: "Tell me what to write in your note."

Terry: "I want my daddy to come back and take me home!"

Teacher jots this down without comment, then reads it back to her, writes her name on it, and places it in a special box for such notes. This seems to work wonders. It helps ease the child's longing and shows how teachers listen and help. The child feels better.

True, plenty of children survive separation without so much tender loving care. They may be expected to start school on their own and to cope without pats, notes, or sympathy. Are they keeping feelings of loss or loneliness hidden inside? Or do they feel quite secure? It's hard to tell. The central question is: Do we know what they are learning *on their own?*

Back to the children who are so distressed during separation and whose teachers go out of their way to help them: Let's ask the same question. Do we know what *they* are learning, not yet on their own? Certainly they learn that teachers are there for them — there to help them cope. They learn that sadness is legitimate and can be channeled into work and play. Teachers "teach" these lessons by being unflappable, by listening and comforting, then by helping the children get busy and productive with materials. Children are learning empathy, respect for others' feelings, and ways to comfort each other. Teachers are setting the example.

Incidentally, other children in the class are not shortchanged. They see and hear how their teachers help other children. They learn what to do and say when they, or other children, feel unhappy.

Children vary. Separation goes easily, proceeds unevenly in fits and starts, or seems endlessly hard. A seasoned teacher may try her patient, good-natured methods over days and weeks and finally reach an intuitive "This is it!" point: "You know, Leslie, you're really OK here. I will help you manage. So come play for a while . . . come with me over here. . . . Let's give the rabbit some fresh water to drink." Or, "Let's go to the kitchen for juice and crackers for the class." Or, "Let's try out that yellow paint at the easel." Whatever . . .

Children gain strength not just from friendly grown-ups. They also gain from using classroom materials, and from playing. Children who are given plenty of time and space for free play will be able to cast off their preoccupation with home and get into pretend play in the housekeeping corner, or with puppets, or out in the yard.

During story time and circle or meeting times, children need a chance to listen to each other's experiences. They pick up perspectives this way and knowledge of how other people get along. Teachers can lead conversation into topics like mothers or fathers going to work, folks traveling to other places by car or airplane, or people moving from one house to another. Circle time is much richer and more educational if focused on the life experiences of children and teachers rather than on merely reviewing the calendar or weather.

Music helps children enjoy themselves and each other — joining in songs, listening, learning finger plays, moving around to music on records or tapes, trying rhythm instruments.

While they work and create with color, shape, texture, line (using

Dena Bawinkel

After a while, children begin to make friends —
the best cure of all for homesickness.

Help from materials and the program . . .

. . . and from friends

Informing parents of progress

Hard times, helpful teachers

David McPherson

Parents like to know which activities and kinds of play have proved especially interesting to their children.

paints and clay and crayons or markers), children are able to express inner feelings.

Table toys serve to focus children who are upset or disorganized. Puzzles, for example, literally are about "putting the pieces together" successfully.

After a time, while exploring materials and trying out activities, children begin to make friends — the best cure of all for homesickness. Even babies and toddlers reach out to each other and seem to enjoy being together.

Teachers keep parents informed about all this, working in partnership with families to help children get used to school. Parents like to know which activities and kinds of play have proved especially interesting to their children and that a friend has been found.

Midday bottles or lunch and naptime may so remind children of their families that they feel somber again. By providing friendly reassurance, teachers help children recover and move ahead much more effectively than by appearing critical, or demanding that children shape up and act their age. (They *are* acting their age!) When children feel upset or uneasy, adult *support* is the key to helping them pull themselves together.

At naptime, a matter-of-fact approach works, though it takes some children a while to relax and rest at school. Teachers feel stressed if too many children cry or misbehave at naptime. Again, the calmest, most professional way works: pats, back rubs, and quiet supervision. Some centers use very soft, low music on tapes or records to provide the nappers with a soothing background. New teachers are advised not to give up when naptime seems to be chaotic, but to keep trying. Eventually, patience and a sure touch win out as children begin to feel at home away from home.

One of the hardest times of day for parent-teacher teamwork is the last hour. The staff member assigned to be the late teacher has the task of maintaining an orderly room and organized program in spite of fatigue and interruptions from arriving parents and departing children. The late teacher must try to remember brief anecdotes to tell parents, find boots and caps, sort out clothing and bottles for the babies, prepare artwork to be carried home, hand out announcements or notes to parents, persuade slow dressers to hurry, even teach children how to dress themselves or push boots onto children who've outgrown them. Teachers must brainstorm these problems and help each other work out smoother solutions — for the children, for their parents, and for themselves. A good lost-and-found system, a special carton for rolled-up artwork, and a large supply of shopping bags help in some centers. So does getting children started on dressing as going-home time approaches (opening a window a little so people don't get overheated). Creative teachers have worked out many solutions. What can go wrong then?

An example of what can go wrong: Mom arrives to fetch Brian. He refuses to put on his coat, he taunts her. The teacher quietly takes charge; it's school turf, not home turf. Because Mom cannot manage Brian right now, the teacher pitches in to help get him ready. She does this without being competitive or showing up the mother as less than capable by chatting casually with her, smiling at her, and then saying good-bye in a friendly way.

Let's look at almost-3-year-old Gina, a girl who gets into power struggles at the point of leave-taking. Dad arrives to take Gina home. Gina's motor goes into high gear. Off she races through the room, inviting a chase. Dad stands there, a mixture of rage and helplessness on his face. He wants to take Gina home *now*. Embarrassing and maddening — terribly hard for the father. And hard for the teacher, too; she has other children to supervise but realizes how difficult this leave-taking is.

End of the Day: Routines, Reunions, Problems

The last hour

Stress at pickup time

Each center needs to establish procedure for the end of the day to ensure order and safety. Some centers say this: As a parent takes his child in hand and says good-bye, he becomes legally responsible for the child.

Problems and solutions

Responsibility

Procedures for pickup

The teacher's mission at day's end is to send children home in reasonable order and good spirits. Parents who (1) are unable to cope with their children, or (2) ask teachers for more detailed information at dismissal time than the usual minute or two of greeting and exchange, or (3) want to stand around visiting with other parents, or (4) let toddlers or other siblings wander through the classroom sampling the wares present practical problems. (1) The teacher needs to have the child partially dressed to go home, ahead of time if at all possible; if not, she may take charge of the dressing when Mom has trouble with it. Over time Brian will learn to dress himself. But right now, the teacher "oils the machinery" by helping out. (2) The teacher recognizes that parents have a right to receive detailed information about their child. She tries to give limited information in a *brief* conversation at leave-taking and at greater length in a note or telephone call later that evening; but not now, and *not in front of the child.* (3) The wish of parents to visit with other parents at pickup time is not peculiar; it is a human need for contact and companionship. But dismissal time from school is not a good time for socializing for more than a minute or two. First and foremost, children need their parents' full attention at this time of reconnection. Moreover, there are practical — even legal — problems with a chatty group of parents. Who is technically responsible for the children? Who is responsible if a brother or sister accompanying a parent destroys materials or gets hurt? Who is responsible for the program continuing in good order if the teacher gets drawn into supervising visiting toddlers?

It seems clear that, for this matter of responsibility at the end of the day, each center needs to establish procedure. Even though parents may feel restricted by it, they will recognize the good sense of ensuring order and safety.

Some centers say this: As a parent takes his child in hand and says good-bye, he becomes legally responsible for the child. He needs to know that. Some parents take a long time to leave — helping their children to crackers from the kitchen, chatting and visiting with each other. In one center this happened: Mrs. S. got her son by the hand on the playground at leave-taking time; she and the boy said good-bye to the teachers and started off. Then Mrs. S. stopped to talk to another parent. Her son ran back into the yard, climbed to the top of the slide, lost his balance, plummeted down the slide, and was injured. In addition to feeling very sorry for the child, the adults had to face the matter of blame and accountability. Who was in charge of this little boy? Teachers assumed that he and his mother were on their way out. The mother may have assumed that, while she stopped to talk, the teachers would refocus their attention on her boy. The insurance agents called in to study the case decided that the mother was responsible; she had announced, child in hand, that they were leaving. The case was dropped. After that unhappy incident, the center set forth clear rules for parents to follow at pickup time.

Assumptions, policies

Even when a parent does make a mistake, holding negative opinions of that parent verges on the harsh and threatens the parent-teacher relationship. Who does not make mistakes? The teacher, at her professional best, remembers that her job is not to categorize parents as "good" or "bad" but is, rather, to (1) provide nurture and education to children and (2) be considerate and supportive of their families. It means the world to children to see and hear teachers responding to their parents with courtesy and respect.

Fair play

There are a few parents who consistently give teachers a hard time, seeming negative or critical. But sometimes a parent has a very legitimate complaint. A single mother, on a tight budget, is understandably angry when, at the end of a long day, her son's new mittens are nowhere to be found. She can't afford this. There are lots of "shoulds" in this situation. The child should learn to keep track . . . the mittens should be labeled . . . the teachers should

"Shoulds"

It means the world to children to see and hear teachers responding to their parents with courtesy and respect.

check the yard and hallway for lost mittens and toys . . . dressing routines should include locating all that the child wore to school that day. The parents, for that matter, should realize that things get lost and that teachers are pulled in many directions.

Such is the stuff of parent-teacher conflict. Solutions exist: Parents can be encouraged to buy iron-on name-labels, or to mark mittens, jackets, boots. Children can be taught during story or circle times how to take charge of their things; teachers and children can check cubbies, hallways, yards for misplaced items. If everyone works together — children, parents, and teachers — instead of resorting to blame, people can learn from one another, help each other, like each other.

Toys from home. Certain children always want to bring a toy from home to school. Some centers discourage it; others think it's good to have toys as "transitional objects." One way: When a toy appears at school in the morning, the teacher admires it, allows it to be shown during breakfast or at circle time. Then it gets parked in a marked teachers' box for departure time. That's the procedure, communicated to all. Allowing personal belongings from home to be played with at school may invite envy, discord, loss, or breakage. If you don't agree with this point of view, you can work out a procedure that makes sense to you. It's the firm, clear policy that counts.

Parents' late pickup. When a parent arrives late to gather up her child, the teacher has had to reassure and occupy the child while they waited together during that last tiring stretch of the day. Many centers set a policy of charging a fine when this happens. Fines seem OK to some parents but impersonal or even offensive to others. The teacher feels she should not be perceived as a baby sitter or hireling — she may well have a family waiting for her at home, or a doctor's appointment, or a class to attend. She cannot be expected to be on call at any hour.

Parents do sometimes have real problems getting to the center by closing time: car trouble, a traffic jam, scheduling mix-ups. At that hour, with feelings of guilt or resentment simmering just below the surface, parents and teachers need to try hard to put themselves in the others' shoes. Perhaps teachers have to go the extra step in these cases — to remain calm and helpful during the final moments of flustered explanations, apologies, and good-byes.

Other Problems: Other Steps

Toys from home

When parents are late

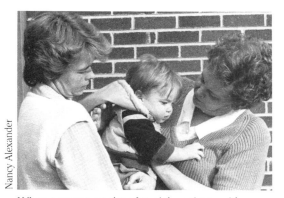

Nancy Alexander

When parents are late for pickup time, with feelings of guilt or resentment simmering just below the surface, parents and teachers need to try hard to put themselves in the others' shoes. Perhaps teachers have to go the extra step in these cases — to remain calm during the final moments of flustered explanations, apologies, and good-byes.

When parents don't arrive at all

What should happen when the parent fails to arrive at all? The teacher is scheduled to close the school. How long should she wait? Where does she take the child when she must finally leave? What measures does the director take with the parent?

Occasionally teachers have crossed over the professional edge into informal, good-neighbor roles — taking children home by car or taxi, or to their own homes. Such solutions have been used only because the teacher was desperate, but they can create very grave problems: people using other people, overstepping boundaries, and causing confusion and worry for children. It is better for parents to develop solid plans for emergencies rather than to call on teachers and aides for extra help after hours.

When children get sick

Centers need to make policies in consultation with the school doctor or local health service on how to handle sick children and ask parents during intake about back-up arrangements at home in case of a child's illness or other crisis.

Sick children. Suzie has coughed all night, has no fever the next morning, seems to be OK at breakfast. Suzie's mother is a lawyer scheduled to appear in court today. Dad is out of town. Mom takes Suzie to the child care center, remembers to mention the cough to the teacher, then rushes off. By noon Suzie has a slight fever, is fussy, and coughs nonstop. What to do? Suzie's mother is unavailable. Suzie needs attention. Furthermore, she is coughing on teachers and other children. Many teachers and parents alike would say that it would be better for Suzie, for the staff, and for the other children if Suzie were at home.

How many times have teachers seen a child brought to nursery school or the child care center looking under the weather? Mom says, on her way out, that her son Fong has been up most of the night with vomiting and diarrhea, but "he seems OK this morning." The next dreaded school epidemic of stomach flu may be about to begin!

What is school policy for Fong and his mother? When *should* a child return to a center after having had diarrhea? ringworm? strep throat? Some pediatricians take a fairly relaxed view about contagious disease in children's settings; others are more conservative. Most centers make their policy in consultation with the school doctor or local health service. Many must follow state regulations. Some simply make their own. Parents need to know the policy. Many directors ask parents during intake about back-up arrangements at home in case of a child's illness or other crisis. Parents may need assistance in planning in advance for emergencies. Not even the healthiest child can avoid an occasional bout with a virus or minor injury. There must be an emergency system for parents to fall back on so that they don't strain parent-school relationships by asking too much of the school.

Regulations regarding medications given to children in preschool centers need to be written down. Is it OK to dispense pills, cough syrup, antibiotics? Who dispenses them? Where are they kept? Has the parent filled out a permission form and signed it? Is the child's doctor or clinic informed and in agreement? These issues cause conflict. They need to be discussed as parents and teachers try to work out sensible, comfortable procedures together. (A helpful book to consult while figuring out your procedures is *A Little Bit Under the Weather*, Fredericks, Hardman, Morgan, & Rodgers, 1986.)

Special treatment. It is wrenching for many parents to give over their child to group care. They have their own ways of caring for their child, their own discipline, their own religion, their own language. They may wonder whether their child will be perceived and treated as their child or only as a member of the school group.

Will Carlos have to go outside even though he is barely over a serious ear infection? Will Mali be helped to stay clear of finger painting today since she has to perform in a dance recital after

Policy

Back-up in emergencies

Medications

David Phillips

Try to say yes to parents' requests if at all possible. Listen analytically; consider consequences; discuss the issues with the director and other teachers.

Parents' wishes for their children

Individual versus group

Positive directions

Preschool as "prep" school?

school? Will Chris be protected from the aggressive little girl who repeatedly bites him at school? Has anyone at the center fixed the splintered wooden climber so dangerous for Rita last week?

A parent's requests of a teacher — to take special note of her child — may be perceived by some teachers as frustrating or irritating and impossible to grant. Parents provide individualized child care at home, in a comparatively small family group. At the center, teachers provide larger group care, often within full classrooms and complicated schedules. They must try to serve children's needs even when they themselves are feeling tired or stressed.

Yet there is a rule of thumb for teachers: Try to say yes to parents if at all possible; at least, *think* about saying yes. Listen analytically; consider consequences; discuss the issues with the director and other teachers. Instead of automatically saying, "I don't believe this! She's asking for special treatment again," consider whether and how the request might be granted. Because of Carlos's history of ear infection, he might spend time in another classroom while his group goes outside. Finger painting for Mali can wait; today she needs to stay superclean. She can crayon. A chronic biter needs a lot of help and limit setting, and the victim and his parents need help and support, too; no doubt about extra teaching effort in that case. The splintered climber should be fixed — perhaps repair can be undertaken by a parent/teacher group. In fact, a system of parent reps working with teachers on school equipment has solved problems in many centers.

Academic curriculum. Some parents request that more academic work be added to a preschool curriculum than presently exists. In one scenario, parents seemed pleased during intake with the developmental program (instead of a highly structured academic one). But then came ambivalence, questions, concerns: "The children are just playing here." "My child already knows all these story books.

18

He knows his numbers and letters. What now?" Or: "Do you realize that these children will be expected to know how to count and write their names by the time they start kindergarten?"

Preschool curriculum is formulated by the director and by teachers, in some places in collaboration with an advisory board. In the developmental approach, children's play activities are viewed as indispensible precursors to the later academic activities of elementary school. They are so described to parents, with snapshots or slides of children working and playing and with vivid anecdotal material shared during conferences and parent-teacher meetings. Films and speakers can elaborate on the theme that children learn through activity; that the "basics" of early childhood are unit blocks, art, puzzles and other fit-together toys and construction kits, story books, dramatic play, music, and the fascinating adventures that go on in preschool science. (See *Developmentally Appropriate Practice in Early Childhood Programs Serving Children From Birth Through Age 8,* NAEYC, 1987.)

Parents' questions deserve generous, clear responses based on current research and on the whole body of knowledge about young children. These responses must also include listening to parents and considering their ideas. Together, parents and teachers can study different learning styles at different ages. They can consider how skills are learned through trial and error, by children and adults alike. They can think about how the learning process evolves as children grow older, and how children's ability to think and reason is as crucial as learning letters and numbers. The subject of how children think and learn is big and complex. All of us need to know more about it.

All of the situations described in these pages have happened recently in actual classrooms; one encounters them in every preschool setting. Part of teaching children is learning from experience,

Responding to parents . . .

Elisabeth Nichols

Parents' questions about the preschool curriculum deserve generous, clear responses based on current research and on the whole body of knowledge about young children. The "basics" of early childhood are unit blocks, art, puzzles and other fit-together toys and construction kits, story books, dramatic play, music, and the fascinating adventures that go on in preschool science.

. . . not sitting in judgment

Working through conflict

Empathy

then being able to predict a problem and come to a solution. What is *not* part of teaching is judging parents harshly, speaking abruptly to them, or dismissing their demands as impossible without really considering parental backgrounds or beliefs. All too often, teachers' day-to-day relationships with parents hit snags because people's experiences and beliefs are so different one from the other.

Early childhood education staff members can learn lessons about conflict resolution from professional trouble-shooters and arbitrators. How do you work to solve problems of accusation, denial, competition over who is right about a child or who is more effective or authoritative? (See NAEYC Ethics Series articles in the March 1985 and May 1987 issues of *Young Children* and follow-up articles in succeeding issues.)

The arbitrator's answer: Listen, analyze, present your own position accurately. Look for common ground, keep talking, promise to think about the issues — and then *think* about them!

For those teachers who are much more comfortable with children than with adults, learning to view the whole human spectrum would help. Parents were once small children too. What sorts of things happened to them? Almost every life has included times of neglect, fear, unjust treatment, and for some, serious trauma, even horrendous damage. It is not always *other people* who suffer from accidents, catastrophic illnesses, robberies or rapes, loss of jobs, drug or alcohol abuse, abandonment. It's people we meet and know, even in children's centers. Though troubles within parents' (and teachers') lives may be hidden from view, they have a powerful effect on children and adults alike. If we, as teachers, extend compassion to everyone, not just to children, parent-teacher relationships will have a chance. It is a professional obligation to try to work sympathetically with the important people in children's lives.

But teachers, too, suffer from anxiety, illness, and stress. Sometimes they may feel that compassion and support are one-sided, always up to them. They're right . . . it can be that way. Part of the job of teaching is to call forth as much poise and warmth as humanly possible and to treat parents well no matter what. Whether or not the parents reciprocate, teachers bear a professional responsibility to work hard to be available and try to understand in order to provide an atmosphere of support, even while holding fast to their own convictions.

Marietta Lynch

For teachers who are more comfortable with children than with adults, it is helpful to learn to view the whole human spectrum. Parents were once small children too.

It is hard to remember the twists and turns of children's progress or problems without records, and one can make serious mistakes trying to reconstruct events without them.

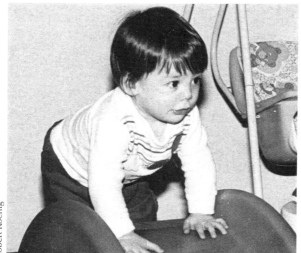

In order to do a first-rate job in education, teachers take on the task of keeping regular, ongoing notes and records about individual children and about the program. These notes are confidential and are specified by law as "working papers." They are in-house records to be used only by staff, thus differentiated from the formal cumulative records that follow children through school and are open to the public on request.

It is hard to remember the twists and turns of children's progress or problems without records, and one can make serious mistakes trying to reconstruct events without them. A few minutes spent each day or so are sufficient. For staff or parent conferences, teachers can read back over their notes to check dates, events, names of children or adults involved in day-to-day episodes. Before a parent conference, the teacher and assistant(s) go over their notes together, refreshing their memories and integrating details and anecdotes to use for planning and highlighting the conference.

On a sober note: It is imperative to keep records of any accidents, injuries, or illnesses during school — date, time of day, witnesses, and an account of just what happened.

When grave problems with a particular child grow to crisis proportion, teachers need to be able to call for — and receive — help from the director and sometimes from consultants trained in areas of classroom discipline or evaluation of children or from specialists in social work or special education. The teachers' records will prove invaluable because they will provide necessary data when assessments and decisions are made.

One great benefit of continuous record-keeping is that it is fascinating and enlightening to read over the notes at the end of a 6- or 12-month period. When did Brian first start to balk at going-home time and refuse to dress himself? What was going on with him in other ways? How did you help him over that hump? What finally worked with Gina so that she became more cooperative with her

Further Steps in Solving Problems

Record keeping

dad? Exactly how often was Fong out sick? Can Chris stand up for himself now instead of always letting himself be a victim? How were you able to help him? When did he begin to change?

A looseleaf notebook works well, with a section for each child in the class. *Of course, it has to be carefully stashed away at school or at home because it is highly confidential.*

Notes about the many daily encounters with parents are important. From the first steps of your relationship, you and the parents have arrived at various stages of cooperation and trust. These steps should be documented in your working papers.

Even though many parents of preschool children are in the work force, there are times when teachers make a special request of a parent to visit the class. One reason for this would be a child having difficulty.

Vicki, age 2½, is biting a lot. Her parents are horrified but don't know what to make of it. The teacher, even knowing that 2s are prone to bite, still feels that this little girl's behavior is exaggerated. She asks the parents whether one of them will come to see how Vicki is managing in school and to help figure out how her biting problem might be solved. The teacher asks the parent(s) to pool strategies with her to help Vicki act and feel less primitive.

Hiroshe still misses his mother long after he began coming to the center. He doesn't seem to have friends. How about inviting his mother to school for lunch to sit with him and see him in action (or inaction) with the other children? She might bring special cookies with her as a treat for everybody. Afterward, at home, Mommy and Hiroshe can reminisce about Miguel who sat next to them at lunch, about the blocks and trucks she saw at school, about the picture Hiroshe had painted — now displayed on the wall near his cubby.

The triad of mother, child, and teacher has taken a step forward.

If they can spare brief periods of time from work, parents may help teachers and children enormously by coming to the center, perhaps even doing something special in the program.

If they can spare brief periods of time from work, parents may help teachers and children enormously by coming to the center, perhaps even doing something special in the program. Rita's mother comes in for a couple of hours to make applesauce with the 4s. Fong's father brings his guitar to the center and plays it for the children after their nap. Suzie's mom always takes time to help out on field trips; she's able to do this because she's self-employed and can arrange her own flextime.

Everyone benefits!

Every center gets into issues of personal preference. The head teacher likes the aide better than the assistant. The volunteer likes Suzie's mother better than any other mom in the troop. Fong's father feels more comfortable with the assistant than with the head teacher. There is nothing remarkable going on here; however, certain standards of fair play have to win out over favoritism. The director (who has to be very careful herself) is in a position to help teachers *talk* out their preferences to prevent them from *acting* them out. She suggests ways for teachers to make sure their behavior with parents is correct.

Say a parent asks the assistant at pickup time for information about his child. The assistant is obliged to respond briefly, but then to relay the question to the head teacher for her response — not because the assistant doesn't have sufficient information or insight to answer but because it is the head teacher who bears final responsibility for the child and the class. This pair — teacher and assistant — might respond to the questions in two quite different ways even though they are in agreement about the child. That would result in confusion and possible conflict.

Inviting parents to visit

Favoritism

Roles acknowledged

Communication between parents and teachers happens all year long — talks by telephone, during social events at school, and during brief, informal encounters in the classroom and on the playground.

Mary Ellen Powers

Conferences

Conversations among director, parents, and teachers go on through the year, as time permits — talks by telephone, during social events at school, and during brief, informal encounters in the classroom and on the playground (and sometimes in the neighborhood grocery store).

Conferences are more formal presentations. Even though some centers do without home visits and limit their parent-teacher conferences to half an hour, many teachers believe that the more time given to parent-teacher discussion the better. Whether compressed into 30 minutes or going into more depth during an hour or so, parent-teacher conferences, in most centers, are held at least once each year, typically twice. Additional conferences may be scheduled for children having trouble. There are many variations of where and when conferences are held: during evening hours, released time, school hours with substitute teachers or volunteers helping in the classroom, or on Saturdays — however people decide to schedule them. Arrangements are not easy. They take extra time and effort. Nonetheless, conferences are regarded as an integral part of education and should not be thought of as impractical or unnecessary.

Decisions have to be made about who comes to the conference. Both parents? Many single parents will have to come on their own or with a relative. In some schools, the director sits in. Some head teachers want to meet parents alone, not including other staff, because they don't wish to overwhelm a parent. Others ask their assistant teachers to sit in on conferences. In extremely difficult conferences, the director may ask an educational consultant or social worker to attend.

Parents often feel anxious about upcoming conferences even when their children seem busy and contented in school. It must be much harder for parents whose children cry and seem sad at school, or are restless and uninvolved or wary and silent, or rush about knocking into people and furniture, or seem to be hitting and biting

For how long?

When?

Who attends?

27

Parents' anxiety

Teachers' approach

Ginger Howard

Give purpose and structure to parent conferences by outlining the main points you want to cover. Fix on one or two goals to aim for as well as on the direction you hope to take in the discussion.

with intensity or rage. Teachers, put yourselves into the shoes of the parents of these children. How comfortable can they be when asked to discuss their children's behavior with you?

First of all, give purpose and structure to the conference by outlining the main points you want to cover — having gone over your notes and talked with other staff members if need be. Fix on one or two goals to aim for as well as on the direction you hope to take in the discussion. Set a professional tone. Also set a social tone with friendliness — offering soft drinks or fruit juice, and displaying some of the child's artwork, snapshots of his block building, or a favorite storybook he loves to hear.

When the parent arrives, the teacher shows the classroom, offers a beverage, and chats informally about the center, perhaps talking for a minute or two about how preschool programs function and the basic philosophy of this curriculum. Next, the teacher begins to speak about the child, recalling how he behaved as he began coming to the center, how he adjusted and became involved, how he made friends, how he came to prefer particular aspects of the program. Recalling from her notes, the teacher illustrates the child's life at school with interesting vignettes.

Now the conference takes a turn. Teacher: "I've been doing all the talking! I really would like to know how you saw Shauna's first days here and then her later adjustment. What kinds of reactions did you see at home?" Perhaps later: "Mrs. S., it helps me so much to hear your descriptions of Shauna and to get a more complete picture of her." Maybe this: "What you're telling me sounds fairly close to our experience with Shauna at school, don't you think?" Or: "Mr. S., what you're saying sounds different from our experience with Shauna here. Does it to you? That wouldn't be unusual; it just sounds as if she's developed different ways of playing and behaving at home and at school. Do you think that poses any problems for her?"

In another moment of the conference, you might say something like this, especially if some disagreement arises: "It would help me work with Shauna if you would tell me more about how she is at home — when the easiest, most peaceful times are for her and for you, and the hard times, too."

Or: "Shauna's experiences at home are the most important of all. Tell me, what seems to work best when she's sad or upset?" Or: "I've described to you our goals for Shauna here at the center. It would be good for me to hear what *you* want her to get out of coming here."

The dialogue progresses and deepens.

Let us suppose such dialogue opens up startling differences — different goals, different styles of discipline, different timetables for learning skills. To work through such situations, the teacher must give the parent time to talk without interruption (within the limits of the schedule) and without argument, no matter how far apart the two viewpoints may be.

Finally, though, the teacher wishes to put into words her contrasting opinions and judgments. You might say: "I'm listening carefully to what you're saying, Mr. M. It's pretty clear that your thinking differs from mine about this matter. I'd like to think over all we have said and to try to spend extra time with your daughter in the classroom if I can manage it. Let's plan to talk again in a month — OK?"

Or: "You know your child, Mr. M. Of course you and your family want this center to meet your expectations. From my corner, I work with numbers of children Sharon's age, and I come to this job with a certain kind of training and experience. . . . I have to be frank with you and say that I see Sharon as needing extra help, from both of us, at school and at home. I hope we can both think about how to work together to give her that help. Let's talk again soon. Maybe we can take a few minutes to talk when you bring Sharon to school next Thursday." (Out in the hall, that is, not in Sharon's presence in the classroom.)

From teacher to parent, and back again

Differences in goals and approaches

Nancy Alexander

To work through differences, the teacher must give the parent time to talk without interruption (within the limits of the schedule) and without argument, no matter how far apart the two viewpoints may be.

In a harder scenario, the teacher may say, slowly and with reflective pauses, "We've talked with you many times about Robert, Mrs. A., and we've tried hard to use your ideas with him. But the truth is that things aren't getting better for him. I must be honest with you; I would be remiss if I were *not* honest. . . . We think that Robert may need special help and that he would benefit from a full evaluation, starting with his own doctor and going from there. It's not so unusual for children his age to be looked at, to find reasons for why they have trouble. The earlier, the better, of course. . . . We would like to ask your permission to talk with Robert's doctor (or clinic), and we might ask our consultant to have a look and advise us about how best to help him. . . . Would you like to think about all this and then give me a call? We need to plan *together* what to do next." When it is unavoidable to speak as strongly as this to a parent, it is crucial not to sound bossy, judgmental, or insensitive.

Sometimes it is not possible for teachers and parents to reach agreement. If we make suggestions gently and respectfully, parents may feel the depth of our concern and decide to go along with our suggestions. It sometimes takes two or three conferences, in addition to brief, informal exchanges, before parents and teachers understand each other's viewpoints, and work jointly on a plan of action. Teacher to director: "Mrs. A. feels strongly, and I disagree with her; but we're finding ways to talk that are a little more open and comfortable. We'll make it."

In the most difficult conferences of all, parents or teachers may decide that the child should be withdrawn from the center. Teachers must remain controlled, fair, courteous. You have done your best — keeping careful records all along and trying in every way to work with the child and the family. Now at an impasse, you express sorrow and regret about what has happened. Invite the child's re-enrollment, if that should seem feasible in the future. Most importantly, the teachers and the director stand firm in their professional judgments and conclusions.

Conferences take parents' and teachers' time and effort — a lot of both. The question is this: Is the alternative (no conferences) acceptable?

There are many parents who have been greatly influenced by talking with a teacher during conferences. Parents have learned about ages and stages of growing children and how their own child's behavior is "normal," though perhaps not easy to handle. They have learned techniques for teaching their child how to become more self-controlled, or more brave, or more creative; and how to enjoy his play and work.

Teachers, for their part, learn details of the child's life in his home and neighborhood — details about which they had no notion before the conference. They gain insight into parental hopes for the child and the parents' interpretation of the child's behavior in the context of their family. Teachers learn about the child as a newborn baby, then as she grew, and finally, as she became ready to start school. With this background information, teachers feel better able to plan for the child and to befriend her.

Obviously, the position in this booklet is that it *is* worth the time and effort to hold conferences with parents and to go the extra mile in many ways — reaching for the highest possible level of your work as a teacher.

Even as I exhort teachers to take extra time and effort in their teaching and in their relationships with parents, and even as I suggest "reaching for the highest possible level of your work as a teacher," I know from experience and observation in the classroom that we all work on various levels of professionalism and dedication. Sometimes we achieve excellence. Sometimes we try and fail. If we feel a commitment to that highest possible level, though, we try again.

Parents gain

Teachers gain

During conferences, teachers learn details of the child's interests and behavior at home and gain insight into parental hopes for the child.

31

As Jimmy Hymes put it:

> *Beyond any question, when you work closely with parents you pay a price. You adjust to the other fellow's ideas, sometimes going faster and sometimes going at a slower pace than you desire. But there are rewards in working together that isolation could never bring. Teachers do gain. Parents gain. And children are the real winners. (1975, p. 4)*

In summary: If we believe, as we say we do, that parents and teachers are both major sources of children's basic knowledge, values, and skills, then we look for ways to build harmonious relationships — to feel empathically for each other, to speak honestly to one another, and to work respectfully with each other — within the realities and constrictions of our disparate styles and goals.

References

Fredericks, B., Hardman, R., Morgan, G., & Rodgers, F. (1986). *A little bit under the weather.* Work/Family Directions, Inc., 200 The Riverway, Boston, MA 02215.

Hymes, J. L., Jr. (1975). *Effective home-school relations* (rev. ed.). Hacienda Press, P.O. Box 222415, Carmel, CA 93922.

National Association for the Education of Young Children (1987). *Developmentally Appropriate Practice in Early Childhood Programs Serving Children From Birth Through Age 8.* Washington, DC: NAEYC.

Suggested by the Author

Bjorklund, G., & Burger, C. (1987). Making conferences work for parents, teachers, and children. *Young Children, 42*(2), 26–31.

Parent involvement [Special issue]. (1985). *Dimensions, 14*(1).

Turner, P. H., Kagan, S. L., & Zigler, E. (1985–86). Parents and caregivers: Allies for children. Unpublished paper, Bush Center in Child Development and Social Policy, Yale University, New Haven, Connecticut.

Wolf, D. (Ed.). (1984, Fall). Parents and teachers [Special issue]. *Beginnings.*

For Further Reading

Especially for teachers

Beard, B., Hunter, B., Lambert, B., & Winters, B. (1986). *The TEA–AEL parent education notebook.* Tennessee Education Association, 598 James Robertson Pkwy., Nashville, TN 37219.

Blau, R., Brady, E. H., Bucher, I., Hiteshaw, B., Zavitkovsky, A., & Zavitkovsky, D. (1977). *Activities for school-age child care.* Washington, DC: NAEYC.

Brady, E. H., Deutsch, D., Farr, K., & Gold, B. (1968). The use of videotapes in parent conferences. *Young Children, 23,* 276–280.

Bredekamp, S. (Ed.). (1987). *Developmentally appropriate practice in early childhood programs serving children from birth through age 8* (exp. ed.). Washington, DC: NAEYC.

Briggs, P. (1985). The early childhood network—We work together for young children. *Young Children, 40*(5), 54–55.

Bromberg, S. L. (1968). A beginning teacher works with parents. *Young Children, 24,* 75–80.

Canady, R. L., & Seyfarth, J. T. (1979). *How parent-teacher conferences build partnerships.* Bloomington, IN: Phi Delta Kappa Educational Foundation.

Cataldo, C. Z. (1987). *Parent education for ealy childhood: Child-rearing concepts and program content for the student and practicing professional.* New York: Teachers College Press, Columbia University.

Dittmann, L. L. (Ed.). (1984). *The infants we care for.* Washington, DC: NAEYC.

Dixon, G. H. (1980). Child development in the family health care center— A painting every time. *Young Children, 35*(3), 49–56.

Frymier, J. (1985). *Methods for achieving parent partnerships: Project MAPP.* Indianapolis Public Schools, 120 E. Walnut St., Indianapolis, IN 46204.

Gordon, I. J. (1976). Parenting, teaching, and child development. *Young Children, 31,* 173–183.

Gordon, I. J., Olmsted, P. P., Rubin, R. I., & True, J. H. (1979). How has Follow Through promoted parent involvement? *Young Children, 34*(5), 49–53.

Gotkin, L. G. (1968). The telephone call: The direct line from teacher to family. *Young Children, 24,* 70–74.

Gotts, E. E., & Purnell, R. F. (1985). *Improving home-school communications.* Bloomington, IN: Phi Delta Kappa Educational Foundation.

Greenberg, P. (1986). *Staff growth program for child care centers.* Acropolis Publishing, 2400 17th St., N.W., Washington, DC 20009.

Harms, T. H., & Cryer, D. (1978). Parent newsletter: A new format. *Young Children, 33*(5), 28–32.

Hayman, H. L. (1968). Snap judgment: A roadblock to progress on parent involvement. *Young Children, 23,* 291–293.

Henderson, A. (Ed.). (1987). *The evidence continues to grow: Parent involvement improves student achievement.* National Committee for Citizens in Education, 10840 Little Patuxent Pkwy., Suite 301, Columbia, MD 21044.

Honig, A. S. (1979). *Parent involvement in early chilhood education.* Washington, DC: NAEYC.

Hunt, D. E. (1987). *Beginning with ourselves in practice, theory, and human affairs.* Brookline Books, Inc., P.O. Box 1046, Cambridge, MA 02238-1046.

Katz, L. G., & Ward, E. H. (1978). *Ethical behavior in early childhood education.* Washington, DC: NAEYC.

Kelly, F. J. (1981). Guiding groups of parents of young children. *Young Children, 37*(1), 28–32.

Marion, M. C. (1973). Create a parent-space—A place to stop, look and read. *Young Children, 28,* 221–224.

McAfee, O. (undated). *Improving school-home communications: A resource notebook for staff developers.* Appalachia Educational Laboratory, Inc., P.O. Box 1348, Charleston, WV 25325.

McCracken, J. B. (Ed.). (1986). *Reducing stress in young children's lives.* Washington, DC: NAEYC.

Nedler, S. E., & McAfee, O. D. (1979). *Working with parents: Guidelines for early childhood and elementary teachers.* Belmont, CA: Wadsworth.

Parent involvement: What your PTA can do. (undated). The National PTA, 700 N. Rush St., Chicago, IL 60611-2571.

Purnell, R. F., & Gotts, E. E. (Eds.). (1987). School-family relations: Issues for administrators [Special issue]. *Education and Urban Society, 19*(2).

Readdick, C. A., Golbeck, S. L., Klein, E. L., & Cartwright, C. A. (1984). The child-parent-teacher conference: A setting for child development. *Young Children, 39*(5), 67–73.

Roopnarine, J. L., & Johnson, J. E. (1987). *Approaches to early childhood education.* Columbus, OH: Merrill.

Souweine, J., Crimmins, S., & Mazel, C. (1981). *Mainstreaming: Ideas for teaching young children.* Washington, DC: NAEYC.

Stevens, J. H., Jr. (1978). Parent education programs: What determines effectiveness? *Young Children, 33*(4), 59–65.

Stone, J. G. (1978). *A guide to discipline* (rev. ed.). Washington, DC: NAEYC.

Swap, S. M. (1987). *Enhancing parent involvement in schools.* New York: Teachers College Press, Columbia University.

Thurlow, A. P. (1972). Parent-teacher communication. *Young Children, 28,* 81–83.

Wenig, M., & Brown, M. L. (1975). School efforts + parent/teacher communications = happy young children. *Young Children, 30,* 373–376.

Zavitkovsky, D., Baker, K. R., Berlfein, J. R., & Almy, M. (1986). *Listen to the children.* Washington, DC: NAEYC.

Frede, E. (undated). *Getting involved: Workshops for parents.* Ypsilanti, MI: High/Scope. (This is a collection of the GPO brochures listed below, including several that are out of print individually.)

Getting involved: Annotated bibliography. (undated). U.S. Government Printing Office. (GPO Stock No. 017-092-00083-9)

Getting involved: Your child and language. (undated). U.S. Government Printing Office. (GPO Stock No. 017-092-00086-3)

Getting involved: Your child and math. (undated). U.S. Government Printing Office. (GPO Stock No. 017-092-00081-2)

Getting involved: Your child and problem solving. (undated). U.S. Government Printing Office. (GPO Stock No. 017-092-00085-2)

Helping children learn self-control. (1986). Washington, DC: NAEYC.

Hymes, J. L., Jr. (undated). *Notes for parents.* Hacienda Press, P.O. Box 222415, Carmel, CA 93922. (This is a collection of 18 brochures, available individually or as a set.)

McCracken, J. B. (1987). *More than 1,2,3: The real basics of mathematics.* Washington, DC: NAEYC.

McCracken, J. B. (1986). *Off to a sound start: Your baby's first year.* Washington, DC: NAEYC.

McCracken, J. B. (1987). *Play is FUNdamental.* Washington, DC: NAEYC.

McCracken, J. B. (1986). *So many goodbyes.* Washington, DC: NAEYC.

Toys: Tools for learning. (1985). Washington, DC: NAEYC.

Brochures especially for parents

Selected NAEYC Publications

If you find this book helpful in your work with young children and their parents, you may want to order other valuable resources from NAEYC as well.

Parents-As-Partners poster/brochure sets (brochures also available individually)

Code #	Title
771	Toys: Tools for Learning
772	Helping Children Learn Self-Control
773	So Many Goodbyes
774	Off to a Sound Start: Your Baby's First Year
775	More Than 1,2,3: The Real Basics of Mathematics
776	Play Is FUNdamental

Other brochures

Code #	Title
518	Finding the Best Care for Your Infant or Toddler
520	Helping Children Learn About Reading
525	How To Choose a Good Early Childhood Program
528	Love and Learn: Discipline for Young Children

Books

Code #	Title
214	Activities for School-Age Child Care
106	Art: Basic for Young Children
132	The Block Book
113	Curriculum Planning for Young Children
224	Developmentally Appropriate Practice in Early Childhood Programs Serving Children From Birth Through Age 8

Books, continued

Two companion books to *Teacher-Parent Relationships*

A Guide to Discipline, also by Jeannette Galambos Stone, is a warm look at how clear expectations, respect for children, and well-planned programs can prevent discipline problems in advance and how calm, firm responses from adults will defuse rather than escalate the problems that inevitably will arise. Code #302

Caring: Supporting Children's Growth, by Rita M. Warren, is a companion book to *A Guide to Discipline.* For parents and teachers to help children as they struggle with the arduous and gratifying tasks of growing up. Code #213